DATE DUE

The SPORTS HEROES Library

Memorable WORLD SERIES Moments

Nathan Aaseng

Lerner Publications Company · Minneapolis

FRONT COVER: All-Star catchers Carlton Fisk (left) of the Boston Red Sox and the late Thurman Munson of the New York Yankees gave fans some memorable World Series moments. They included Fisk's winning home run in game six of the 1975 Series and Munson's three-series total of 25 hits and .373 average, third highest in World Series history. Photo by Peter Travers.

ACKNOWLEDGMENTS: The photographs are reproduced through the courtesy of: pp. 4, 10, 13, 18, 21, 34, 45, 50, National Baseball Hall of Fame and Museum, Inc.; pp. 6, 8, 27, 29, 31, 36, 38, 40, 42, 48, 52, 55, 57, 58, 60, 63, 64, 67, 69, 70, 73, 76, 78, Wide World Photos, Inc.; p. 59, Pittsburgh Athletic Company, Inc.

To Brian

LIBRARY OF CONGRESS CATALOGING IN PUBLICATION DATA

Aaseng, Nathan.
  Memorable world series moments.

  (The Sports heroes library)
  Summary: Highlights great moments in the history of baseball's World Series from 1912-1975.
  1. World series (Baseball)—History—Juvenile literature. [1. World series (Baseball)—History. 2. Baseball—History] I. Title. II. Series.
  GV863.A1A27   796.357'782   81-13725
  ISBN 0-8225-1073-1   AACR2

Manufactured in the United States of America

International Standard Book Number: 0-8225-1073-1
Library of Congress Catalog Card Number: 81-13725

1 2 3 4 5 6 7 8 9 10 92 91 90 89 88 87 86 85 84 83 82

Contents

Lou Gehrig congratulates Babe Ruth after one of baseball's most memorable moments. The Bambino had just hit the famous "called" home run in game three of the 1932 World Series.

Introduction

More than any other sporting event, there is something about the World Series that sticks in the minds of fans. Even baseball fans with the foggiest memories will often turn into walking encyclopedias of information when it comes to the World Series. They never talk about a Series "back in the 1930s" or one that happened "a few years ago." Instead they talk about the "1932 Series" or "the Dodgers and the Yankees in 1955" as clearly as if they just happened yesterday.

Perhaps one reason that the World Series is so memorable is because it was the first major pro championship. The World Series began in 1903 when Pittsburgh of the National League agreed to meet Boston of the new American League in a battle of the league champions. Boston won five of eight games to claim the title. The following

This was the scene at the start of baseball's first World Series in 1903 at Boston's Huntington Avenue Baseball Grounds. That year the immortal Cy Young, who had a 28-9 record, led Boston to two Series wins and compiled an ERA of 1.59 in 34 innings.

year, the New York Giants of the National League refused to play Boston in the World Series because of grudges they still held against the American League. But the contest was continued in 1905, and it has been held every October since then.

Another reason why the World Series is so special is because of the suspense of matching two top teams that have not played each other all year. The World Series is the only time teams from the American and the National leagues meet because baseball, unlike other major sports, does not allow interconference play during the regular season.

Finally, baseball seems to be tailor-made for championship play. Though it is a team sport, it is also a series of individual match-ups: pitcher vs. batter, runner vs. thrower, fielder vs. the ball. Since there is really no action away from the ball, the spectator is able to see all of these match-ups. Fans get a chance to see great players show their skill in key, pressure-packed situations.

These exciting match-ups have produced striking performances in the World Series from the very start. The 1905 Series showed three Hall of Fame pitchers at their best. Every one of the five games was a shutout by either Christy Mathewson or Joe McGinnity of the New York Giants or Chief Bender of the Philadelphia A's. Mathewson stood up to the pressure best and threw three scoreless games. Since then, the World Series has had a history of being both thrilling and unpredictable. In fact, if a person tried to dream up all the wild and fascinating things that could happen in a game, he or she would still fall short of matching some of the best World Series.

The pressure of standing alone in the spotlight of a seven-game World Series has given baseball a rich history of heroes and goats. It has made household names out of little-known reserves and has

Christy Mathewson (left) matched arms with Chief Bender in the 1905 World Series. Bender shut out the Giants in game two and finished the Series, 1-1, with a 1.06 ERA. Mathewson, in a supreme individual performance, pitched three shutouts to lead New York to the championship, four games to one.

turned great players into legends. And it has turned a good many October dates into unforgettable moments of baseball at its best.

8

1
Boston vs. New York
1912

The 1912 World Series probably should have been played under a circus tent rather than on a ballfield. Never has the game of baseball seen such a series of blunders, thrills, comedy, and confusion. The ballplayers chipped in for a total of 31 official errors. But even the fans made an unusual mistake. One day many of them left the ballpark believing that the losing team had really won!

It was an unlikely cast of skilled players who were caught in that madhouse. The Boston Red Sox had posted a record of 105-47 while taking the American League pennant. That was a league record for wins that stood until 1931. The Red Sox

Hall of Famer Tris Speaker led the Red Sox with a .383 average in 1912. During the 1912 Series, his .300 average paced the Boston attack.

featured outstanding defensive play in their outfield, which included Harry Hooper, Duffy Lewis, and Tris Speaker. Speaker not only played center field as well as anyone in history, he also hit for a lifetime average of .344. Boston's pitching was led by 22-year-old sensation Smokey Joe Wood. His nickname had been earned with a blazing fastball, a pitch that also accounted for 10 shutouts and a 34-5 record that season.

Their opponents, the New York Giants, were managed by the successful John McGraw. McGraw's men had been as impressive as Boston, winning 103 and losing 48. And their pitching was even more reliable than Boston's. Hurling for the Giants were the great Christy Mathewson (hero of the 1905 Series), Hall of Fame pitcher Rube Marquard, and the National League's earned run average (ERA) champ, Jeff Tesreau.

As expected, the Series started off with a tense pitchers' duel between Wood of the Red Sox and Tesreau of the Giants. New York led 2-1 in the seventh before Boston scored three runs to take a 4-2 lead. The Giants closed the gap to 4-3 in the ninth inning and then put runners on second and third base. But Smokey Joe Wood fired his fastball for two strikeouts to win the game.

Things started to get sloppy in the second game. Christy Mathewson suffered through five errors by his teammates and had all he could do to hold the Red Sox to six runs. The Giants also scored six runs and by the time the game had moved into the 11th inning, it was too dark to continue. The game was declared a tie.

The Giants were counting on Rube Marquard to pull them even in the next game. He came through, holding Boston to five hits until the ninth inning. Clinging to a 2-0 lead, Marquard gave up a single to Duffy Lewis and a double to Larry Gardner. A typical Giant error then put runners on second and third base with two out, and the score now 2-1.

Darkness and fog were beginning to cover the stadium as Marquard threw to the next batter. Boston's Forrest "Hick" Cady belted the pitch deep to center field. Centerfielder Josh Devore raced into the gloom near the fence to try to catch the ball. He was deep in the fog when he finally caught the ball for the final out of the game. Since the Giants' clubhouse was beyond the outfield fence, Devore saw no reason to come back to the infield. He disappeared with his catch into the Giants' outfield clubhouse.

Meanwhile the Red Sox fans had seen the Boston

In 1912 nobody fired a baseball faster than Boston's Smokey Joe Wood. That year he struck out 21 Giants in 22 World Series innings for three victories. While Smokey Joe never regained his 1912 pitching form, he finished his career as an outfielder with a respectable .283 batting average.

runners cross home plate, and they did not know that Devore had made the catch. They assumed the ball must have fallen for a hit, and they left the park celebrating a 3-2 win. It must have been a shock when they opened their newspapers and found that New York had won, 2-1!

Smokey Joe Wood made certain there was no

confusion about the next game. He breezed to a 3-1 win, striking out eight and walking no one. One game later, Christy Mathewson of the Giants tried his luck again against Boston's Hugh Bedient. Mathewson gave up only five hits, but this time it was his team's hitting that let him down. Boston won the game, 2-1, to take a three-games-to-one lead in the Series.

Again Marquard came to the Giants' rescue and beat the Red Sox, 5-2, in game six. The loss did not bother Boston, though, because they expected Joe Wood to win the Series the next day. But before that game could get started, there was an argument in the outfield stands. The Red Sox had sold more tickets than they had seats. It happened that their most loyal fans, who called themselves the "Royal Rooters," were the ones who had been kicked out of their seats to make room for the others. But the Royal Rooters did not leave peacefully. They tore down part of the outfield fence before they were finally chased out of the stadium.

The half-hour delay to repair the fence ruined Wood's warm-up. After sitting around all that time, he could not throw with his usual speed. The Giants ripped into his fastball and bombed the Red Sox, 11-4, to tie the Series.

The Boston fans were so upset at the treatment of the Royal Rooters that many of them stayed away from the park on the final day of the Series. But those who did go to the game saw a wild finish. New York took an early 1-0 lead and threatened to widen the gap in the sixth inning. Then Boston's Harry Hooper threw himself over the outfield fence while going after a long Giant hit. The Boston fans helped Hooper keep his balance, and he caught what could have been an important home run.

The Red Sox finally scored off Christy Mathewson in the 7th and brought in Smokey Joe to finish the game. He and Mathewson battled through several scoreless innings before the Giants broke through for a run in the 10th inning.

Mathewson then strode to the mound, confident that he could protect his 2-1 lead. He got the first batter to lift a soft fly ball to outfielder Fred Snodgrass. But out number one suddenly vanished when Snodgrass dropped the ball. Even Fred's fine catch on the very next play could not make up for that terrible error.

Mathewson, frustrated by fumbling teammates throughout the Series, then started making some mistakes of his own. He walked a batter, and that brought the Red Sox top hitter, Tris Speaker, to the plate. Fortunately, Mathewson got Speaker to pop up near the first base foul line. Unfortunately, he called for the *wrong* man to field the ball!

Mathewson signaled that the catcher was in the best position to catch the ball, but the first baseman was actually much closer. The first baseman backed away, and the catcher scrambled to try and reach the ball. But he could not get there in time, and the Giants had let another out slip away from them.

Speaker turned to Mathewson and said, "That play will cost you the game." True to his word, he rapped a hit to score the tying run. Larry Gardner then followed with a long fly ball to bring in the winning score.

In that game Mathewson had again pitched brilliantly without getting a victory. Wood won his third game of the Series as the Red Sox escaped with the title. But even the Red Sox fans had to agree that if baseball was to survive as a serious game, it could not stand many more championships like the 1912 Series.

2
Washington vs. New York
1924

If any player deserved to win a World Series, it was Walter Johnson of the Washington Senators. He has been called the greatest pitcher of all time, winning 416 games and throwing 113 shutouts in his career. Walter had such fine control of his bullet-like fastball that he did not even need another pitch, such as a curveball. Johnson was also known as much for his politeness as for his skill. For much of his career, he was known as "Big Swede." (He later admitted that he was Dutch-German rather than Swedish, but he had not pointed out the error before because he did not want to offend any Swedes.)

Walter Johnson, the Big Train, toiled with the lowly Washington Senators for 17 seasons—including 11 in which the Senators lost more games than they won—before capturing a pennant. Johnson's record of 416 career wins is the second highest in baseball history. Only Cy Young won more.

It was Walter's bad luck to spend most of his career with terrible teams. Johnson lost 26 games in which he had allowed only one run. Not until his 18th year in the major leagues, in 1924, did his team win a pennant. By that time, Walter's skills were beginning to fade. Still he had posted a 23-7 record that year and had won the American League's Most Valuable Player award. Baseball fans across the country hoped that Walter had enough of a fastball left to finally win a World Series title.

Washington's opponents were McGraw's New York Giants. They scored often with a balanced attack headed by Frankie Frisch, Bill Terry, Hack Wilson, Ross Youngs, and 18-year-old third basemen, Fred Lindstrom. If there were any doubts as to whom would be the villains of the Series, the Giants quickly erased it. They were almost barred from the Series because of an attempted bribery by one of their players in a late season game.

As everyone had expected, Washington started Johnson in the first game. The Giants found it hard to hit his pitches, and 12 of them were called out on strikes. But when Bill Terry and George Kelly did connect with his fastball, they hit home runs. With little support from his own batters, Johnson went into extra innings with the score tied at 3-3.

Washington's bats continued to fail, and Johnson finally lost the game in the 12th by a score of 4-3.

Washington took a 3-1 lead into the ninth inning of the second game and promptly lost it. But shortstop Roger Peckinpaugh drove home the winning run for the Senators in their half of the inning for a 4-3 win.

The Senators did not have to worry about getting chewed out by their manager for their third game loss. Manager Bucky Harris, who also played second base, had no one to blame but himself. In one inning he had had a perfect chance to kill a Giant threat when a double-play ball was hit to him. But Harris messed up the play, and the Giants took the lead and went on to win, 6-4.

Goose Goslin took charge of game number four for Washington. He banged out four hits, including a home run, to spark his team's 7-4 win.

Walter Johnson was back in the next game for another chance at his long-awaited World Series win. The man who gave Walter the most trouble that day had been only an infant when Johnson started pitching pro ball. Eighteen-year-old Fred Lindstrom collected four hits off the veteran pitcher. Johnson also made the mistake of giving up a home run to the opposing pitcher, Jack Bentley. New

Rookie Fred Lindstrom rapped Senator pitching for a team-leading 10 hits during the 1924 Series.

York won, 6-2, and Walter trudged off in defeat again. Baseball fans sadly realized that he would not get another chance to start a game in the Series.

Then the Giants sent pitcher Art Nehf to finish off the Senators in game number six. But Senator pitcher Tom Zachary, who later suffered unwanted fame as the man who gave up Babe Ruth's 60th home run in a season, was the better pitcher that day. Manager Harris redeemed himself for his earlier error by driving in two runs with a double.

They were the only runs that Zachary needed as he held the Giants to one run.

As the seventh and final game approached, Bucky Harris worried about the Giants' slugging left-hander, Bill Terry. Terry was murder on right-handed pitchers and had batted .429 through the first six games. He was usually benched against left-handed pitchers but, unfortunately, Washington's top pitchers were right-handed.

Harris finally came up with a clever plan. He started right-hander Curly Ogden and, as expected, New York put Terry into the lineup to bat against him. Ogden pitched to two batters and then startled the Giants by walking off the mound as Terry came to bat. Washington brought in lefty George Mogridge, and New York responded by replacing Terry with a pinch-hitter. Mogridge pitched until the sixth inning and then left in favor of right-hander Fred "Firpo" Marberry. The purpose of all of the shuffling was to get Terry out of the game so that Washington could use their right-handers. The Giants had walked right into the trap!

Manager Harris not only used his head. He surprised his team by using his muscle, too. After hitting only one home run all season long, Harris hit his second home run of the World Series in the fourth inning of the final game. But New York charged back with three runs in the sixth to take a 3-1 lead. All those cheering for Johnson's Senators felt depressed. After waiting for so many years, it hardly seemed fair that this fine man would finish the Series without a win.

A whole career's worth of bad luck, however, evened out for Walter Johnson in just one game. The Senators loaded the bases in the eighth inning with two out. The next batter then sent what looked like an inning-ending ground ball to third base. The ball suddenly hit a pebble and took a crazy hop over Fred Lindstrom's head, scoring two runs to tie the game.

In the 9th inning, 36-year-old Walter Johnson got the call to try to shut down the Giants. With the winning run on third base, he fired a third strike past George Kelly to get out of trouble. Through the 10th, 11th, and the first half of the 12th inning, he matched the scoreless pitching of Jack Bentley. Washington, as usual, could not seem to get a run when he needed it.

Muddy Ruel came to bat for Washington in the last of the 12th with one out. He popped an easy foul over the catcher's head. But Giant catcher Hank Gowdy stumbled over his face mask, and the ball fell as a harmless foul. Ruel then doubled, and Giant shortstop Travis Jackson booted a ground ball to put runners on second and third. The final blow came when Earl McNeely hit another ground ball to third base. Lindstrom squared himself to field the ball and then stared open-mouthed as the ball again hit a pebble and took a weird bounce. It bounded over his head into left field, and the Senators scored the winning run in a 4-3 game.

If it had not been for the fact that the bad breaks made Walter Johnson a winner, people would have had to feel sorry for the Giants. After watching the disasters of the seventh game, one Giant shrugged that a New York win, "wasn't meant to be." Walter Johnson finally had his World Series win, even if it had taken a catcher's mask and two pebbles to get it for him.

3
New York vs. Chicago
1932

Fans across the country flocked to see New York Yankee slugger Babe Ruth in action during the regular seasons. With his all-around play, Ruth usually gave them a spectacular show. He led the American League in home runs 12 times, averaged 50 home runs a year from 1926 to 1931, boasted a lifetime batting average of .342, and was known for his accurate throwing arm. He also had been a fine pitcher in his early days, leading the league in earned run average in 1916 when he pitched for Boston.

But Ruth saved his most devastating performances for the World Series. The greater the pressure, the more he seemed to enjoy himself. In the 1918 World Series, he set a record that lasted for 43 years when he pitched 29-2/3 consecutive scoreless innings. He batted .625 in the 1928 World Series and pounded a total of 15 Series home runs in his lifetime.

For a team to try and put pressure on Ruth during a World Series was suicide. In 1932 the Chicago Cubs made the mistake of putting Ruth on the spot. The result was a moment that helped to make Ruth the most talked-about player of all time.

The New York Yankees had rolled into the 1932 World Series at the height of their power. Ruth had hit 41 home runs that year, and Lou Gehrig, 34. With fine seasons from second baseman Tony Lazzeri and catcher Bill Dickey, the New York team coasted to a 107-47 record.

The Chicago Cubs of the National League offered strong opposition. Their lineup was loaded with three Hall of Fame hitters: Kiki Cuyler, Billy Herman, and Gabby Hartnett. The Cub pitching staff seemed powerful enough to make the Yankee sluggers work for their runs. Lon Warneke sported a 22-6 record with a 2.37 ERA, Guy Bush was 19-11, and Charlie Root, 15-10.

Shortstop Mark Koenig as a Yankee. As a Chicago Cub, Koenig faced his old mates in the 1932 World Series.

This, however, was not the usual friendly World Series rivalry. During the year, the Cubs' regular shortstop, Billy Jurges, had been injured. The Cubs then traded for Mark Koenig to take his place. Koenig did a tremendous job, and his clutch hitting and fielding were largely responsible for the Cubs' first-place finish. The Cubs, however, had only

27

voted him one-half share of their World Series' earnings. Their penny-pinching angered the Yankees, who had known Koenig well from his days as the Yankee shortstop.

The Cubs had to file through the Yankee dressing room to get to the field for the first game of the Series. It was here that the name-calling started, long before the first pitch was thrown. And as the Series went on, the name calling would get worse.

Chicago pitcher Guy Bush started off with three perfect innings in the opening game. He later probably wished he had quit while he was ahead! The Yankee hitters began to take out their anger on the Cubs with a three-run fourth inning, high-lighted by Gehrig's home run. Then they pushed across five more runs in the fifth. With such batting help, Yankee pitcher Red Ruffing had no trouble in beating Chicago, 12-6.

Next came the only game of the Series that even resembled a pitching duel. Pitcher Lon Warneke kept the game reasonably close for the Cubs. But they could manage only two scores off Lefty Gomez and lost by a 5-2 margin.

The defeats made the insults sting even worse for the Cubs. By the time the Yankees arrived in Chicago for the next game, the Chicago writers and

Lou Gehrig, the Iron Horse, gets into shape for another season. Gehrig's record of playing in 2,130 consecutive games in 14 seasons stands as one of the greatest achievements in the history of the sport.

fans joined their players in stepping up the feud. The sportsmanship at the ballpark for game number three was disgusting, with nonstop insults flowing the entire game. It had no effect on the Yankee sluggers, though, as Ruth and Gehrig both homered early. The score was tied 4-4 when Ruth came to bat in the fifth inning, showered with jeers and catcalls from the Cub bench. He took two strikes from Charlie Root and then stepped out of the batter's box.

There are many versions of what happened next. Some players claimed that Ruth merely held up one finger, saying that it only took one to hit it. Others say he pointed to the hecklers in the Cub dugout. But most observers insisted that Ruth backed away from the plate and stared into the Cub dugout. Enjoying a chance to make the Cubs eat their words, he pointed straight out to the center field stands as if to say that he would hit a home run on the next pitch.

Some of the small black newspapers in Chicago gave an even more interesting version of what happened. They said a man named Loudmouth Latimer went to all Cub games to heckle the opposing team from his center field seat. Most players dreaded having to put up with Latimer for a whole game, and Loudmouth had been especially hard on Ruth that day. When Ruth fielded a ball poorly in the outfield, Latimer had thrown lemon peels at him. Ruth then pointed a warning finger at the loudmouthed fan. According to this account, when Ruth backed away from the plate, he had pointed to Latimer in center field.

Whatever, Ruth stepped back in to face Root. Even though the pitch was thrown low, Ruth swung and golfed a home run deep into the center field stands at just about the spot he had been pointing to. Babe enjoyed a romp around the bases while the Cub dugout stared on in silence. Had he really been

Babe Ruth finishes his trot around the bases after homering in the first inning of game three in the 1932 Series. Four innings later, the Sultan of Swat poked the home run that he predicted he would hit.

so bold as to predict his home run? Ruth himself did not give his version of what had happened. But the moment has served to strengthen the reputation of the legendary Babe Ruth. Almost forgotten in the uproar about Ruth's hit was the fact that Lou Gehrig immediately followed with another home run. That proved to be the winning hit in a 7-5 victory.

Following the game, baseball commissioner Kenesaw Mountain Landis ordered the two teams to clean up their behavior. The Cubs and the Yankees obeyed the order, and tempers cooled for the fourth game. The Yankee bats were as hot as ever, though. After Chicago had taken a 4-1 lead in the first inning, New York roared back. Tony Lazzeri supplied two home runs, and the Yankees won another one-sided romp, 13-6. They had completely thrashed a good Chicago team in four straight games.

The Yankees finished the Series with a team batting average of .313 and a total of eight home runs in four games. Lou Gehrig had enjoyed a fabulous Series, hitting .529 and slugging three home runs. But the star of the 1932 World Series was clearly Babe Ruth. Chicago had learned the hard way how difficult it was to get the best of Ruth, especially at World Series time.

4

St. Louis vs. Detroit

1934

Neither the Detroit Tigers nor the St. Louis Cardinals had been expected to make it to the 1934 World Series. That is, unless one counted the opinion of Dizzy Dean. Dean, the Cardinals' All-Star pitcher, had almost no formal schooling. He loved to talk, joke, and brag, and he generally lived up to his nickname. When his brother Paul (sometimes called Daffy by the press) joined the team in 1934, Dizzy announced that the pennant race was over. He said that "me and Paul" would win 45 games between them, and that the season should be a breeze. During one doubleheader, Dizzy had a no-hitter until the eighth inning of the first game. Paul then pitched

As a rookie in 1934, Paul Dean won 19 games for the Cardinals. Combined with brother Dizzy, the Deans won 49 games to lead St. Louis to the pennant. Paul, never as flamboyant as his older brother, neither liked nor fit the Daffy nickname that sportswriters tagged on him.

a full, nine-inning no-hitter in the second game. "If I'd of known Paul was going to pitch a no-hitter, I'd of pitched one, too," said Dizzy.

Despite Dean's confidence, winning the pennant

was not a breeze for St. Louis player-manager Frankie Frisch. Not only did he have to put up with the Deans who threatened to walk out in midyear, he also had the largest collection of pranksters in baseball. Led by Pepper Martin, they staged fistfights in hotel lobbies, spitting out popcorn as if it were teeth, and went through Harlem-Globetrotter-style warm-ups before games. Typical of the headaches they gave Frisch was when shortstop Leo Durocher decided to get married during the last week of a tight pennant race. But with 30 wins from Dizzy and 19 from Paul, the Cardinals were the National League champs.

Detroit, while not so playful, was an even bigger surprise. The team had finished in fifth place in the American League the year before. But trades for Mickey Cochrane and Goose Goslin improved the club instantly. These two, along with a usual fine year from second baseman Charlie Gehringer, and great seasons from newcomers Hank Greenberg and Schoolboy Rowe, helped set up a World Series date with St. Louis. Greenberg had batted in 139 runs, while pitcher Rowe had won 24 of 32 decisions, including 16 in a row.

As usual, Dizzy Dean had so much confidence that he could hardly understand why Detroit bothered to

Detroit's Lynwood "Schoolboy" Rowe won 24 games in 1934, his best season in baseball. The big hurler beat the Cardinals in game two of the Series but lost, 4-3, to Paul Dean in game six.

show up for the game. Although his boasts made him few friends, they did make believers. Dean set down the Tigers in the first game by a score of 8-3. Five errors by the Detroit infielders had helped to smooth the way. And Joe Medwick had taken care of the St. Louis offense with four hits, including a home run.

It was Detroit's turn to pitch their ace in the second game, and Schoolboy Rowe did not let them down. Even though he only gave up two runs in 12 innings, he still needed some shoddy fielding by St. Louis to give him a 3-2 victory. Wild Bill Hallahan and Bill Walker of St. Louis pitched well enough to deserve a shutout, but some missed fly balls sent them down to defeat.

The younger of the Dean boys had to live up to his brother's bragging in game number three. Living dangerously, Paul allowed Tiger baserunners almost every inning. But the young rookie pitched out of trouble and beat Detroit, 4-1. Pepper Martin had hit a double and a triple to pace the Cardinal attack.

Neither of the Deans were scheduled for action the next day. But Dizzy had decided this was going to be the Deans' Series. When manager Frisch looked at his bench in the middle of the game to find a pinch runner, he was told to look at first base. There stood Dizzy, who had already decided he would be the baserunner. Frisch decided to give in this time, and he let Dean have his way. But that was a decision that nearly cost St. Louis the Series.

When Pepper Martin hit a ground ball, Dean ran hard toward second base. Trying to force a bad throw from the second baseman, Dean did not slide into the base. Instead the throw from the fielder caught him solidly on the head and knocked him cold.

An unusually serious Dizzy Dean scores a St. Louis run in the Series finale. Although Detroit had averaged more than six runs per game throughout the season, Dizzy and Paul held the hard-hitting Tigers to fewer than four runs in each of their five Series games.

Dean was carried off the field unconscious and was rushed to the hospital. Detroit, meanwhile, romped to a 10-4 win behind the hitting of Hank Greenberg.

The next day the Tigers were stunned to see Dizzy Dean grinning at them from the pitching mound. Proving that he was fully recovered, he pitched a fine game. His one mistake was serving up a home run ball to Charlie Gehringer in the sixth inning. That was enough to send Dizzy to defeat as Detroit's Tommy Bridges beat him, 4-1.

After that defeat, the odds did not look good for St. Louis. Detroit needed to win only one of the next two games, and they were matching their best pitcher, Rowe, against rookie Paul Dean. But again Paul came through, beating Rowe by a score of 4-3. Not only did he pitch well, he also batted in the winning run in the seventh inning.

With only one game left to decide the Series, the Detroit fans tried to give their team some help. Hoping to keep the Cardinals awake all night, they circled the Cardinals' hotel in a sound truck. But the St. Louis team that took the field for the seventh game looked anything but tired.

In game seven Dizzy Dean was back on the mound, trying to make good on his promise of an easy win. And this time he made no pitching mistakes.

Joe "Ducky" Medwick slides hard into third as Tiger third baseman Marv Owen steps aside. Medwick and Owen ended the play by fighting and nearly starting a stadium riot.

He also must have been impressed with his brother's batting performance, because he came out swinging on his batting turns. Dizzy slashed two hits in one inning as the Cardinals scored seven times! After that the outcome of the game was never in doubt, especially since Dean was pitching.

The game and the Series should have ended quietly with the Cardinals' easy win. But trouble started when Cardinal Joe Medwick collided with Detroit third baseman Marv Owen while running out a triple. Owen fell on top of Medwick, and the two fought for a few seconds. When the inning was over, Medwick returned to his defensive position in left field. There he made an ideal target for hundreds of angry, frustrated Detroit fans. They pelted him with fruit, vegetables, and bottles until the outfield looked like a dump. Medwick finally thought it best to retreat, and he waded through the garbage back to the Cardinal bench.

Baseball commissioner Landis decided to play it safe rather than fair, and he ordered Medwick thrown out of the game! The Cardinals were shocked at the order but since they had such a large lead, they went along with it. Medwick left, the Tiger fans stopped throwing things, and St. Louis finished the game and the Series with an 11-0 win.

The Dean boys had been responsible for all four St. Louis wins. Dizzy finished with a Series record of 2-1 and a 1.73 ERA. Paul topped that with a 2-0 mark and a 1.00 ERA. As Dizzy had predicted, the Cardinals' win had been truly a family affair.

The Yankee Clipper, Joe DiMaggio, crosses home plate after the first of his two home runs in the 1947 World Series.

5
New York vs. Brooklyn
1947

There can be no better way for a ball player to finish his career than as a World Series hero. For players such as Bill Bevens and Al Gionfriddo, who had struggled hard to stay in the major leagues, a spectacular World Series would have been a special thrill. Each of these players had a chance for glory beyond his wildest dreams in the last game of his career. One of them came close, only to fall to a crushing defeat. The other succeeded. And their extraordinary efforts changed the 1947 World Series from one of the dullest to one of the most memorable.

Even though none of their pitchers won as many as 20 games, the New York Yankees had won the American League pennant that year by 12 games.

The Yankees, as usual, had not needed great pitching. Center fielder Joe DiMaggio was considered such a great player that even though Boston's Ted Williams had led the league in batting, home runs, and RBI's, Joe had been voted the league's Most Valuable Player. With able support from outfielder Tommy Henrich and catcher Yogi Berra, the Yanks entered the World Series with a 97-57 record.

The Brooklyn Dodgers, their opponents, had no superstars on their team. They were just beginning to develop the talent of players such as Jackie Robinson and Pee Wee Reese—players who would make the Dodgers a powerhouse for the next decade. Still they had won the National League crown with a 94-60 mark. A large audience tuned in the first World Series ever televised to see if the Dodgers could challenge their crosstown rivals.

It took the Yankees almost five innings to solve the pitches of Brooklyn's 21-game winner, Ralph Branca. But they struck quickly in the fifth inning and scored five runs to send Branca out of the game. New York's Spec Shea earned the victory, while reliable reliever Joe Page finished the 5-3 contest. Yankee pitcher Allie Reynolds needed no help in the second game. He struck out 12 Dodgers and waltzed to a 10-3 victory.

Yogi Berra, star Yankee catcher and outfielder during the 1940's, 1950s, and 1960s, holds World Series records for games played (75), at-bats (259), hits (71), and doubles (10). Appearing in 14 Series, Berra also hit 12 home runs. This placed him just behind two other Yankee greats, Mickey Mantle and Babe Ruth.

Until then, the Series had not shown its first television audience anything to interest them in the game of baseball. But things began to get interesting in the third game. Then Brooklyn scored six runs in the second inning and spent the rest of the game

trying to hold off Yankee rallies. Yogi Berra brought New York close when he hit the first pinch home run in Series history. But Brooklyn's relief specialist, Hugh Casey, finally stopped the Yankees for a 9-8 win.

There was no reason to suspect that there would be any less scoring in game number four. The Yankees were so short on pitching that they started Floyd "Bill" Bevens. Despite good hitting support, the chunky right-hander had managed only a 7-13 record in the regular season.

New York tried to get Bevens a huge lead in the first inning. No one was out when DiMaggio walked with the bases loaded to score a run. The Dodger relief pitchers, however, stopped New York from scoring any more that inning. Meanwhile the Dodger batters were doing nothing against Bevens. Inning after inning went by without a Dodger hit. Only the pitcher's unusual wildness allowed Brooklyn to score. The Dodgers squeezed out a run on two walks, a sacrifice bunt, and an infield ground out. As the game went into the late innings, it became obvious to everyone in the ballpark that Bevens was close to completing the World Series' first no-hitter.

By the time Bill warmed up to start the ninth inning, the tension was almost unbearable. He held a 2-1 lead and needed only three more outs for his no-hitter. The crowd gasped as Brooklyn's Bruce Edwards lashed a long drive to the outfield, but the ball was caught for the first out. Bevens then walked Carl Furillo, giving up his ninth free pass. When Spider Jorgenson fouled out for the second out, the Yankees could hardly wait for the last Dodger hitter to bat so they could celebrate with Bevens.

At that point, there was a slight delay in the game when Brooklyn sent in reserve outfielder Al Gionfriddo to run for Furillo. As Bevens then turned his attention to the Dodger batter, Pete Reiser, Gionfriddo dashed for second base. A good throw from catcher Yogi Berra would have gotten Gionfriddo for the final out. But the Yankee's hopes were jolted when the Dodger barely slid safely under a high throw.

A battle of wits followed as the managers sought to gain an advantage. New York's Bucky Harris ordered Bevens to walk Reiser to bring Eddie Stanky to the plate. Brooklyn's Burt Shotton then sent veteran Cookie Lavagetto to pinch hit for Stanky. Lavagetto had batted only 69 times all season. He was well known as a pull hitter, and the Yankee fielders swung around to the left side of the field when he batted. But the old Dodger chose that time to hit one of his rare line drives to right field instead. Outfielder Tommy Henrich frantically dashed toward

Labels on photograph: DI MAGGIO, PINELLI, STIRNWEISS, HENRICH, McQUINN, McGOWAN, PITLER, RIZZUTO, MIKSIS, GIONFRIDDO, BEVENS, BERRA, LAVAGETTO, BLADES, GOETZ

A never-to-be-forgotten World Series moment. This photograph shows where players and umpires were when Dodger pinch-hitter Cookie Lavagetto broke up Bill Bevens' no-hitter with two out in the ninth of game four. Yankee right fielder Tommy Henrich, who had moved to right center field, had no chance to catch Lavagetto's drive (circle) before it hit the wall (X).

the right field foul line but could not get to the ball. It soared over his head for a hit and bounced off the wall. By the time Henrich grabbed the ball and returned it to the infield, two runs had scored to give Brooklyn a 3-2 win. Bevens, who had come within one pitch of a no-hitter, walked off the field as the losing pitcher. After the Series, he would never again appear in a major league game. The outcome seemed even more unjust when Hugh Casey, who had thrown only one pitch, was named the winning pitcher.

The Yankees recovered from their disappointment to win the fifth game, 2-1. DiMaggio's fifth inning home run and strong pitching by Spec Shea were all the Yankees had needed.

The Dodger hitting attack finally got going in the sixth game. Then Brooklyn grabbed an 8-5 lead midway through the game and then sent in 5-foot, 6-inch reserve Al Gionfriddo to the outfield. Though a poor hitter, Gionfriddo was a speedy outfielder, and Brooklyn wanted his defensive ability to help them hold their lead.

In the sixth inning, the Yankees made their move to finish the Series. There were two men on base when DiMaggio lashed a line drive headed for the left field bleachers. Gionfriddo sped after it, jumped in the air with his back to home plate and somehow grabbed it before it disappeared over the fence, 415 feet from home plate.One of the Yankee runners, thinking the ball could not be caught, had run as fast as he could around the bases. The relay throw from the outfield easily caught him for a double play to end the Yankee rally. Gionfriddo's catch had saved the game and Brooklyn won, 8-6.

New York spoiled the Dodger performance by winning the final game, 5-2. In that game Tommy Henrich got the key hit, and Joe Page came on to

Al Gionfriddo makes the greatest catch in World Series history. His miraculous play in game six robbed Joe DiMaggio of a home run and sent the Series into a seventh game.

pitch the final five innings. But few people remember that final game. In fact, the 1947 World Series may have been one of the few championship contests in which the losers are remembered more than the winners. Bevens, the losing pitcher, and Gionfriddo, from the losing Dodger team, each left baseball with a final, unforgettable memory in his final season.

6
Pittsburgh vs. New York
1960

Few teams have taken as terrible a beating as the Pittsburgh Pirates did in the 1960 World Series. New York pounced on Pirate pitching for a .338 team average, 10 home runs, and 55 runs—all World Series records. The Pirates managed only a .256 average, 4 home runs, and 27 runs. But there was no need to pity the poor Pirates. For when the dust had settled from the Yankee attack, Pittsburgh had somehow managed to win the title!

Led by shortstop Dick Groat, the National League's batting champion and Most Valuable Player, the Pirates were a solid team. They also had fine all-around players, such as second baseman Bill

Pirate shortstop Dick Groat completes the game-ending double play over sliding Yankee Tony Kubek in Pittsburgh's 6-4 win of the 1960 Series opener.

Mazeroski and outfielders Bill Virdon and Roberto Clemente. Their pitching was excellent with 20-game winner Vern Law and 18-game winner Bob Friend in charge. And if either should fail, they still had baseball's top reliever, Elroy Face, to bail them out.

Challenging them was a typical hot-hitting, average-pitching Yankee team. Mickey Mantle and Roger Maris, the American League's best power hitters, anchored the lineup. Surrounding these two were other feared hitters such as Yogi Berra, Bill Skowron, and Elston Howard. Their pitching did not scare anyone, and Art Ditmar's 15-9 record was the best among their starters. Yet they had scored enough runs to win 15 straight games heading into the World Series.

In the first inning of the Series, the Pirates greeted Ditmar with a shower of hits. The Pirate attack had sent Ditmar to the showers before most fans had settled into their seats. Bill Mazeroski's fourth-inning home run provided a further boost for Pittsburgh. Though outhit 13-8 in the game, they held on to win, 6-4. Elroy Face had relieved Vern Law to protect the lead.

The Pirates, however, never had a chance in the second game. The Yankees scored points faster than a pinball machine, with seven runs in the sixth inning alone. Mickey Mantle's two home runs were just 2 of the 19 New York hits in a 16-3 romp.

New York then continued to keep its opponent on the run. The Yankee doing the most damage was weak-hitting Bobby Richardson. The little second baseman matched his season total for home runs with a bases-loaded clout in the third game. He then added two more RBI's for a total of six. New York pitcher Whitey Ford, who had not pitched well that season, found his form in the Series. He made things even more embarrassing for Pittsburgh by shutting them out on four hits that game. The Yankees won, 10-0, and seemed likely to run away with the championship.

Vern Law was called in to restore order in game number four. He stopped the one-sided nonsense and aided his own cause with a run-scoring double. Bill Virdon then singled in two more, but it was almost not enough. The Yankees put two men on base in the seventh. Bob Cerv then followed with a 400-foot drive to center field. Virdon had to make a leaping grab to stop the Yankee rally. Pittsburgh's trusty reliever, Face, then retired the last eight batters to save a 3-2 victory.

New York then gave Ditmar a chance to get even for his poor first game performance. But in the fifth

Pittsburgh relief specialist Roy Face saved three Pirate victories against the powerful Yankees in the 1960 Series.

game, he lasted less than two innings before being replaced. Pittsburgh's Harvey Haddix breezed through the Yankee lineup until the late innings. Again the Pirates called on Elroy Face to protect their lead. Face pitched to eight batters and got them all out as the Pirates won, 5-2.

The Yankees, however, came out slugging again in the sixth game. Their power continued to be supplied by little Bobby Richardson. He hit two triples and boosted his World Series runs-batted-in total to a record 12. Whitey Ford enjoyed another relaxing afternoon of pitching, blanking the Pirates for the second time, this time by a score of 12-0. The Yankees must have wished they could have used Ford in one of the closer games!

It seemed to the Pirates that they had to jump out to an early lead if they were to have any chance against New York. Rocky Nelson provided that early spark with a first-inning home run off Bob Turley. By the end of the second, Pittsburgh had stretched its lead to 4-0, and they threatened to get back at the Yankees for those earlier embarrassing losses.

But Bill Skowron homered in the fifth for New York. When the Yankees threatened again the next inning, Pittsburgh decided to take no chances. They brought in Face to finish the game. Face seemed a safe bet to win the Series, having retired 18 of the last 19 hitters to bat against him. But his streak ran out when Yogi Berra hit a three-run home run off him. It was obvious that Face did not have his usual magic as the Yankees took a 5-4 lead and then built it up to 7-4 by the eighth inning.

The Pirate half of the eighth inning was a flashback to 1924. Pittsburgh had one man on base when a double-play ball was hit right at sure-handed shortstop Tony Kubek. But the ball took a wicked

Injured Yankee shortstop Tony Kubek gasps for air after being struck by a bad-hop grounder.

hop and caught the Yankee fielder in the throat, knocking him to the ground. New York pitcher Jim Coates then made matters even worse when he forgot to cover first base on a ball fielded by the first baseman. Pittsburgh took advantage of these events to move ahead, 9-7, with their key hit a home run by reserve catcher Hal Smith. In the ninth, however, the Yankees came right back to tie the score.

When the game moved into the bottom of the ninth, New York right-hander Ralph Terry was pitching. Right-handed batter Mazeroski stepped in

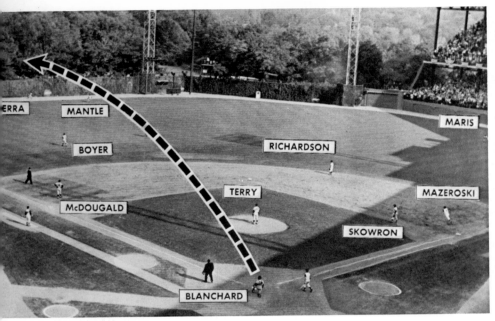

A frustrated New York team looks on as Bill Mazeroski's Series-winning home run sails into the left field stands.

to try his luck against him and finished the Series the way he had started it in the first game. With one powerful swing, Mazeroski clubbed a home run over the wall for a 10-9 win.

The Pirate fans celebrated wildly as Mazeroski circled the bases for Pittsburgh's first championship in 35 years. And the Yankee sluggers walked off the field in defeat. They must have wondered what more was expected of them before they could win the World Series.

Downtown Pittsburgh after the Pirates' World Series win

Cincinnati's Pete Rose slides headfirst into third in 1972 World Series action while Oakland's Sal Bando makes a late tag.

7
Oakland vs. Cincinnati
1972

If the Cincinnati Reds had been told that they would win the 1972 World Series by getting the Oakland A's reserve catcher out, they would have felt pretty confident. As it turned out, all they would have had to do was walk that second-string player. Then they would have won the title in five or six games.

Nobody could have predicted that Fury Gene Tenace would dominate a World Series as it had never been dominated before. Tenace had sat on the bench behind Dave Duncan most of the year. He had caught only 49 games and had batted a poor .225 with only five home runs. And in the play-offs just before the Series, he had been Oakland's easiest out. Against the Detroit Tigers that week, Gene had managed just one hit in 17 trips to the plate for a .059 average.

With such a mediocre record, Tenace hardly seemed to belong on the same field with the Big Red Machine lineup of Cincinnati. Johnny Bench was the National League home run champ and Most Valuable Player. And Pete Rose, Joe Morgan, Tony Perez, and Bobby Tolan were all among the game's top hitters.

The shaggy-haired A's seemed like amateurs next to the hard-hitting, clean-cut Reds. Only left fielder Joe Rudi, with a .305 average, had inched over the .300 mark in hitting. And Oakland's main home run threat, Reggie Jackson, was not even able to suit up for the Series after breaking his leg sliding into home in the play-offs. The A's were putting their hopes on a strong pitching staff that included wiley Catfish Hunter and Ken Holtzman, fireballers Vida Blue and Blue Moon Odom, and reliever Rollie Fingers.

In the first game, however, the A's weak hitting attack received help from an unexpected source. It was startling enough when Gene Tenace hit a home run his first time up. But when he did it again his second time up, baseball fans across the country

Gene Tenace rips his first of four World Series home runs. This one in the second inning of game one gave Oakland two runs.

were asking the same question: Who is Gene Tenace, and where did he come from? Oakland collected only two more hits and no more runs the entire game. But Tenace's hits were enough to give Oakland a 3-2 win as Holtzman and Blue combined to keep the Cincinnati hitters away from the plate.

Most fans, however, figured that Tenace had been very lucky in the first game. So they were not surprised when he faded into the background in the

Jim "Catfish" Hunter mowed down the Reds on six hits in Oakland's 2-1 win in game two. Hunter, who won 21 games for the A's in 1972, finished the Series with two wins and no losses in 16 innings.

next two games. Game number two belonged to Joe Rudi. That underrated outfielder helped his team to a 2-1 lead with a home run. The Reds were still having trouble hitting the A's pitching, with Catfish Hunter and Rollie Fingers doing the work.

64

Cincinnati's Denis Menke finally got ahold of a pitch in the ninth inning. But Rudi made a game-saving grab against the left field wall to win the game.

Those first two low-scoring games were slugfests compared to the third game. Then Oakland's Blue Moon Odom struck out 11 and allowed only one run. But his performance still was not good enough. Even the game's lone run should probably not have scored because the Reds' Tony Perez slipped rounding third base on a base hit. But Oakland shortstop Bert Campaneris had assumed that Perez would score easily on the play, so he did not pay attention to him. Perez scored, and Cincinnati won, 1-0, behind pitcher Jack Billingham.

Now was the time for Gene Tenace to prove that his first game heroics had been no fluke. In game number four, Gene ripped his third Series home run off Don Gullett to stake his team to an early 1-0 lead. The pitching had been so overwhelming in the Series that even that slim lead seemed safe. Then Ken Holtzman shut out the Reds for seven innings, but he was replaced in the eighth by a fresher pitcher, Fingers. Manager Dick Williams probably had second thoughts about that move after the Reds scored two quick runs off Fingers.

Trailing by a run in the ninth, Oakland decided

to take a lesson from Tenace. They dusted off a string of seldom-used players to see if they would have the same luck against the Reds that Tenace was having. Sure enough, pinch hitter Gonzalo Marquez got a hit. Tenace then stroked a single to move Marquez along. Pinch hitter Don Mincher also hit safely, scoring Marquez with the tying run.

The A's must have decided it would be foolish to stop a good thing. Next they sent yet another pinch hitter, Angel Mangual, to the plate. As he slapped a single to score the winning run, Mangual made it a perfect inning for the Oakland benchwarmers.

Cincinnati's Pete Rose got his team going by hitting the first pitch of game number five for a home run. Then Oakland's Tenace matched that with his fourth of the Series. In the ninth inning, Rose finished what he had started by driving in the winning run off Fingers. Still Oakland came within a whisker of tying the game in the ninth when pinch runner Odom was called out at home on a close play.

Baseball fans who were turning into nervous wrecks because of five straight tense ballgames finally got a breather in the sixth game. Then the Reds at last found a pitcher they could hit, blasting Vida Blue for an 8-1 victory.

In an exciting climax to game five, Cincinnati's All-Star catcher Johnny Bench blocks the plate and tags out A's pinch runner Blue Moon Odom. The play preserved the Red's 5-4 victory and kept them alive in the Series.

The final game matched the two tough pitchers from game number three, Odom and Billingham. The two, pitching as strongly as before, dueled through five innings with the score at 1-1. Then Oakland's only run was driven in by none other than Tenace. He hit a grounder that bounced off a seam in the artificial playing field and then bounced high over the reach of the infielders.

Blue Moon Odom could have used some of

Tenace's luck. Despite another great performance, he had to leave the game with the score still tied at one run apiece. Oakland manager Dick Williams was as nervous as everyone in the stands and made a total of 12 trips to the mound to talk with his pitchers. In the sixth inning, Oakland's Campaneris reached third base with Tenace coming up. By this time, the Reds should have known better than to pitch to Gene. Tenace made them pay for their mistake by hitting a double to score Campaneris with the lead run. Sal Bando followed with another double to make it 3-1.

Meanwhile the Reds got one last look at many of the Oakland pitchers. Hunter, Holtzman, and Fingers all came in to throw a few pitches past the Reds. When Pete Rose flied out to Joe Rudi in the ninth inning, it was all over. The A's had won another close game, 3-2.

Gene Tenace had batted .348 for the Series with four home runs and nine runs batted in. The rest of his team put together hit .197 with one home run and seven runs batted in. Other than Tenace, no Oakland player had driven in more than one run. Obviously, the Reds' pitchers had prepared well for the Oakland batters. But Gene Tenace had caught them and the whole baseball world by surprise.

The A's win the Series! Oakland manager Dick Williams runs out to congratulate his jubilant players, including Sal Bando (top), Rollie Fingers, and catcher Dave Duncan.

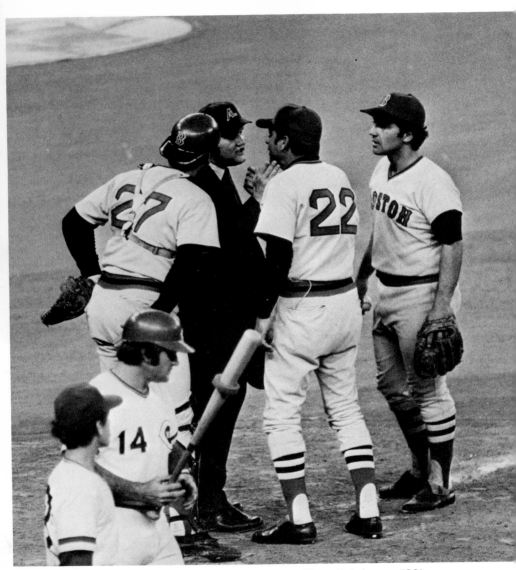

Red Sox catcher Carlton Fisk (27), manager Darrell Johnson (22), and third baseman Rico Petrocelli argue with umpire Larry Barnett over a controversial play in game three of the 1975 World Series.

8
Cincinnati vs. Boston
1975

The 1975 World Series could not have come at a better time. Baseball was losing fans to other sports, such as football. Some people were writing off baseball as an old-fashioned game that was too dull for modern taste. But there was nothing dull about the Boston-Cincinnati clash in 1975. The sixth game in particular has been called the best championship game ever played. It kept millions of Americans up past midnight, waiting to see how it would end. The late inning tension, key hits, and great fielding plays made the 1975 World Series one long advertisement for the game of baseball.

The Cincinnati Big Red Machine was moving into high gear in 1975. The Reds had won 108 games during the year and had swept the Pirates in three games in the play-offs. Their lineup of Rose, Morgan, Foster, Perez, Bench, Griffey, Geronimo, and Concepcion was one of the top collections of hitters that had ever been put together on one team. Manager Sparky Anderson shuffled his pitching staff in and out of games as if they were models in a fashion show. With Don Gullett (15-4) leading the way, the pitchers were always well rested and able to get the job done.

When the Boston Red Sox had added a pair of rookies to their team that year, it was like winning two sweepstakes prizes on the same day. Jim Rice had batted .309 and hit 22 home runs. The only reason he had not won the American League Rookie of the Year crown was because his teammate Fred Lynn had been even better. Lynn was an excellent center fielder who had hit .331 with 21 home runs. Together with veterans Carl Yastrzemski and Carlton Fisk, they made opposing pitchers dread traveling to Boston. And the short left field fence at Boston made pitchers feel even more unwelcome.

Except for Luis Tiant, the Red Sox had found it just as nerve-wracking to pitch in the small park.

Veteran Luis Tiant shut out Cincinnati on five hits in game one and singled and scored the contest's first run.

The well-traveled Cuban with the curious wind-ups did not seem to be bothered by anything. He had led Boston to an upset sweep of their play-off series with the three-time champion A's.

Despite a deep supply of hitters on both sides,

the first Series game remained scoreless through six innings. The old master Tiant and the hard-throwing Gullett pitched marvelously until Boston broke through for six runs in the seventh. Tiant continued to frustrate the Reds and allowed only five hits in a 6-0 win.

Game two was another unexpected pitching duel as Bill Lee took a 2-1 lead into the ninth inning. After Johnny Bench doubled, the Red Sox called on reliever Dick Drago. Drago retired two men before Concepcion singled, scoring Bench. Concepcion stole second and then scored on Griffey's double for a 3-2 Cincinnati win.

The big bats started connecting in the third game, and six home runs sailed over the fences of Cincinnati's Riverfront Stadium. The last of those was driven out by Boston's Dwight Evans in the ninth inning when the Red Sox rallied to tie the game, 5-5. The Reds threatened in the tenth inning and sent pinch hitter Ed Armbrister to the plate. He tapped a bunt in front of the plate. Boston catcher Carlton Fisk could not get around Armbrister to field the ball, and that cost his team the winning run. The Red Sox were furious that no interference was called on the play, but the game was awarded to Cincinnati.

Down two games to one, Boston again turned to Tiant. Now Luis had to work harder than he had in the first game. He got himself in and out of trouble throughout the game and dodged disaster long enough to record a 5-4 win.

As game number five got under way, Cincinnati's Tony Perez was struggling with a reputation as an automatic out at the plate. He had been retired in each of his 15 trips to the plate in the Series. But Perez found his old hitting touch in that game and hit two home runs. Don Gullet then held off the Red Sox attack to earn a 6-2 victory.

For the next several days, the sports pages were filled with weather reports. The players tried to find some way to pass the time as rain washed out play for three straight days. But when game six finally started, it proved to be worth the long wait. Fred Lynn started the action with a three-run first inning home run.

Then the Red Sox took advantage of the three-day rest to bring Luis Tiant back for another performance. But Tiant had reached the end of his tricks for that year. The Reds hit him hard in the fifth inning. Not only did they score three runs to tie the game, they almost made Fred Lynn a permanent part of the center field wall. Lynn tore

Bernie Carbo (far right) is embraced by his Boston teammates after hitting the game-tying, three-run homer in game six, a game many baseball fans say was the most thrilling ever played. Carbo, a former Red, turned Fenway Park into a madhouse with his tension-filled pinch hit.

after a line drive by Ken Griffey and almost shook the entire stadium when he crashed full speed into the wall. While Lynn did not catch the ball, he survived the collision and stayed in the game.

Cincinnati, however, kept putting points on the scoreboard. Two runs in the seventh and a run in the eighth on Geronimo's home run made the Red

Sox fans ready to give up on the Series. But in the bottom of the eighth, Boston put two men on base with pinch hitter Bernie Carbo batting. Carbo had two strikes on him when he was fooled by a pitch. He lunged awkwardly at the ball and tipped it just enough to foul it off and avoid a strikeout. Then he guessed right on the next pitch and launched a game-tying home run.

Boston nearly ended the game in the ninth inning when they loaded the bases with no one out. But when Lynn fouled to George Foster on a shallow fly ball, Denny Doyle stunned his teammates by trying to score. He was easily thrown out at the plate, the rally was over, and the game went into extra innings.

Defense again came to the rescue as the Reds threatened to end the Series in the 11th. With a runner on first, Joe Morgan smashed what looked to be a game-winning hit. But Dwight Evans raced after the ball, snared it on the run, and fired back to first base for a double play.

Cincinnati then called on their seventh pitcher of the game, Pat Darcy, to pitch the 12th inning. Boston's Carlton Fisk made sure Darcy was the last pitcher of the game when he drove a pitch for a home run. The Red Sox catcher whooped and galloped around the bases, jumping on home plate

Carlton Fisk about to be mobbed by the Red Sox after hitting the dramatic, game-winning homer in the 12th inning of game six

to end the game at 12:34 in the morning. The Red Sox organist summed up the feelings of the fans when he played the "Hallelujah" chorus.

In contrast to the hard-fought game six, the final game started off as if the Reds were going to give the game away. Don Gullett could not find home plate, and he walked in two runs. Boston's Bill Lee protected a three-run lead until late in the game. Then as the Reds were beginning to challenge him, he had to leave the game with a blister on his pitching hand.

The Reds rallied to tie the score at 3-3 going into the ninth inning. The final blow hardly did justice to exciting hits and plays that had filled the Series. With two out in the ninth, Joe Morgan blooped a single just over the infield to bring home the winning run.

The Reds celebrated as much from relief as from joy. Manager Sparky Anderson best described what had happened in this most thrilling Series. "We proved we're the best team in baseball," he smiled. "But not by much."

World Series Games

Series winners are listed first. American League teams are shown in italics.

1903	*Boston*/Pittsburgh	1945	*Detroit*/Chicago
1905	New York/*Philadelphia*	1946	St. Louis/*Boston*
1906	*Chicago*/Chicago	1947	*New York*/Brooklyn
1907	Chicago/*Detroit*	1948	*Cleveland*/Boston
1908	Chicago/*Detroit*	1949	*New York*/Brooklyn
1909	Pittsburgh/*Detroit*	1950	*New York*/Philadelphia
1910	*Philadelphia*/Chicago	1951	*New York*/New York
1911	*Philadelphia*/New York	1952	*New York*/Brooklyn
1912	Boston/New York	1953	*New York*/Brooklyn
1913	*Philadelphia*/New York	1954	New York/*Cleveland*
1914	Boston/*Philadelphia*	1955	Brooklyn/*New York*
1915	Boston/*Philadelphia*	1956	*New York*/Brooklyn
1916	Boston/Brooklyn	1957	Milwaukee/*New York*
1917	*Chicago*/New York	1958	*New York*/Milwaukee
1918	*Boston*/Chicago	1959	Los Angeles/*Chicago*
1919	Cincinnati/*Chicago*	1960	Pittsburgh/*New York*
1920	*Cleveland*/Brooklyn	1961	*New York*/Cincinnati
1921	New York/*New York*	1962	*New York*/San Francisco
1922	New York/*New York*	1963	Los Angeles/*New York*
1923	*New York*/New York	1964	St. Louis/*New York*
1924	*Washington*/New York	1965	Los Angeles/*Minnesota*
1925	Pittsburgh/*Washington*	1966	*Baltimore*/Los Angeles
1926	St. Louis/*New York*	1967	St. Louis/*Boston*
1927	*New York*/Pittsburgh	1968	*Detroit*/St. Louis
1928	*New York*/St. Louis	1969	New York/*Baltimore*
1929	*Philadelphia*/Chicago	1970	*Baltimore*/Cincinnati
1930	*Philadelphia*/St. Louis	1971	Pittsburgh/*Baltimore*
1931	St. Louis/*Philadelphia*	1972	*Oakland*/Cincinnati
1932	*New York*/Chicago	1973	*Oakland*/New York
1933	New York/*Washington*	1974	*Oakland*/Los Angeles
1934	St. Louis/*Detroit*	1975	Cincinnati/*Boston*
1935	*Detroit*/Chicago	1976	Cincinnati/*New York*
1936	*New York*/New York	1977	*New York*/Los Angeles
1937	*New York*/New York	1978	*New York*/Los Angeles
1938	*New York*/Chicago	1979	Pittsburgh/*Baltimore*
1939	*New York*/Cincinnati	1980	Philadelphia/*Kansas City*
1940	Cincinnati/*Detroit*	1981	Los Angeles/*New York*
1941	*New York*/Brooklyn		
1942	St. Louis/*New York*		
1943	*New York*/St. Louis		
1944	St. Louis/*St. Louis*		